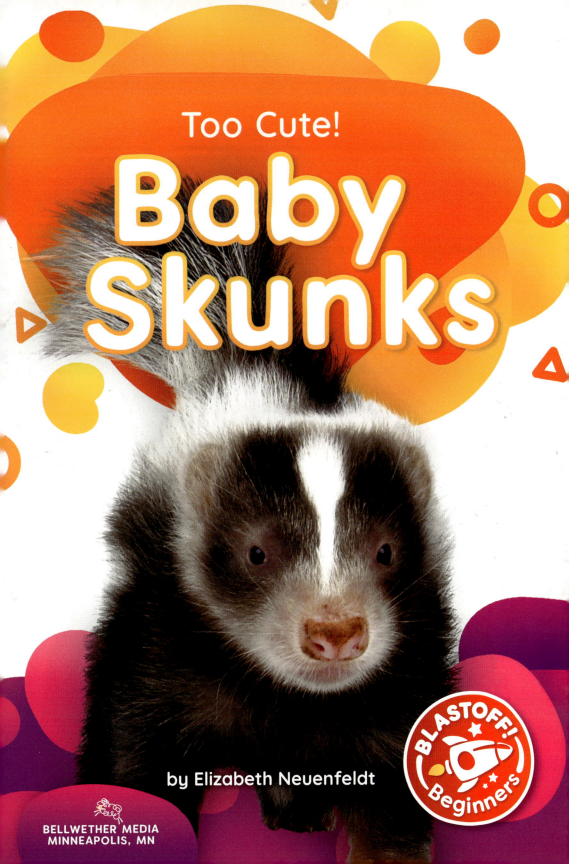

Blastoff! Beginners are developed by literacy experts and educators to meet the needs of early readers. These engaging informational texts support young children as they begin reading about their world. Through simple language and high frequency words paired with crisp, colorful photos, Blastoff! Beginners launch young readers into the universe of independent reading.

Sight Words in This Book

and	get	jump	the	when
are	go	look	their	
at	have	many	they	
by	in	play	this	
eat	is	run	time	
find	it	soon	to	

This edition first published in 2024 by Bellwether Media, Inc.

No part of this publication may be reproduced in whole or in part without written permission of the publisher. For information regarding permission, write to Bellwether Media, Inc., Attention: Permissions Department, 6012 Blue Circle Drive, Minnetonka, MN 55343.

Library of Congress Cataloging-in-Publication Data

Names: Neuenfeldt, Elizabeth, author.
Title: Baby skunks / by Elizabeth Neuenfeldt.
Description: Minneapolis, MN : Bellwether Media, 2024. | Series: Blastoff! Beginners: Too Cute! | Includes bibliographical references and index. | Audience: Ages 4-7 | Audience: Grades K-1
Identifiers: LCCN 2023039891 (print) | LCCN 2023039892 (ebook) | ISBN 9798886877748 (library binding) | ISBN 9798886878684 (ebook)
Subjects: LCSH: Skunks--Infancy--Juvenile literature.
Classification: LCC QL737.C248 N48 2024 (print) | LCC QL737.C248 (ebook) | DDC 599.76/81392--dc23/eng/20230825
LC record available at https://lccn.loc.gov/2023039891
LC ebook record available at https://lccn.loc.gov/2023039892

Text copyright © 2024 by Bellwether Media, Inc. BLASTOFF! BEGINNERS and associated logos are trademarks and/or registered trademarks of Bellwether Media, Inc.

Editor: Betsy Rathburn   Designer: Jeffrey Kollock

Printed in the United States of America, North Mankato, MN.

Table of Contents

A Baby Skunk!	4
Play and Spray	6
All Grown Up	18
Baby Skunk Facts	22
Glossary	23
To Learn More	24
Index	24

A Baby Skunk!

Look at the baby skunk. Hello, kit!

Play and Spray

Newborn kits are tiny. They have many **siblings**.

siblings

newborn kit

Kits stay in **dens**. They drink mom's milk.

Soon, kits go outside. They stay by mom.

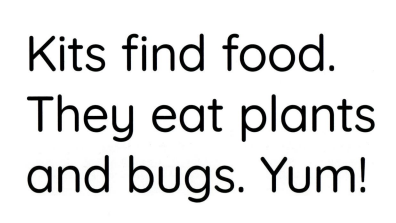

Kits find food. They eat plants and bugs. Yum!

Kits play!
They run
and jump.

Kits **spray** when they get scared. It stinks!

spraying

All Grown Up

Kits get bigger.
Their fur
gets fluffy!

This kit is grown.
Time to
leave home.
Bye, mom!

Baby Skunk Facts

Skunk Life Stages

newborn · kit · adult

A Day in the Life

stay by mom

find food

play

Glossary

dens

homes for kits

newborn

just born

siblings

brothers and sisters

spray

to shoot out a stinky liquid

To Learn More

ON THE WEB

FACTSURFER

Factsurfer.com gives you a safe, fun way to find more information.

1. Go to www.factsurfer.com.

2. Enter "baby skunks" into the search box and click .

3. Select your book cover to see a list of related content.

Index

bugs, 12
dens, 8, 9
drink, 8
eat, 12
food, 12
fur, 18
home, 20
jump, 14
milk, 8
mom, 8, 10, 11, 20
newborn, 6, 7
outside, 10
plants, 12
play, 14
run, 14
scared, 16
siblings, 6
skunk, 4
spray, 16, 17

The images in this book are reproduced through the courtesy of: reptiles4all, front cover, p. 1; Nynke van Holten, pp. 3, 4, 22 (kit); Chris Brignell, p. 5; Debbie Steinhausser, pp. 6, 17; All Canada Photos/ Alamy, pp. 7, 22 (newborn), 23 (newborn); Evelyn D. Harrison, p. 9; Don Johnston/ Alamy, p. 11; badahos, p. 12; Minden Pictures/ SuperStock, p. 13; Debbie Steinhausser/ Alamy, p. 15; critterbiz, p. 19; Holly Kuchera, p. 21; Eric Isselee, p. 22 (adult); Danita Delimont Creative/ Alamy, p. 22 (stay by mom); Karel Bock, p. 22 (find food); Design Pics/ Alamy, p. 22 (play); Jus_Ol, p. 23 (dens); agefotostock/ Alamy, p. 23 (siblings); DavorBozo, p. 23 (spray).